Penguin Parade

Emma Lynch

Penguin Power

How much do you know about penguins? They're black and white, they waddle along the ice and they're cute and funny – right? In fact, there's much more to find out about these amazing animals. Penguins move very quickly, and are good hunters. They can live in some of the coldest places in the world. In this book you will meet a family of penguins and find out about their lives.

As you waddle through these pages, write down and keep your answers to each **QUIZ** *question. (Remember, the answers are in the book!)*

Penguins are birds, but they cannot fly.

Pick of the Penguins

Penguin Parents

Time to meet Mum and Dad ...

PAGES 6 TO 9

Penguin Patrol

Don't forget to look after the egg!

PAGES 10 TO 13

Penguin Pile-Up!

It's time to huddle up.

PAGES 14 TO 15

Penguin Play

The chick grows up and has some fun!

PAGES 16 TO 19

Pole to Pole

Find out some fun facts!

PAGES 20 TO 23

Penguin Parents

Meet Mum and Dad. They are Emperor penguins. Emperor penguins live in the seas around Antarctica, near the South Pole. In winter, they move onto the open ice to breed. Mum and Dad live in a group of Emperor penguins, called a colony.

Antarctica is one of the coldest places on Earth. Emperor penguins are the only animals to live in Antarctica over the winter.

Emperor penguins can grow as tall as a four-year-old child!

Emperor penguins have a bill for eating and flippers for swimming. They can dive deeper than any other seabird. Emperor penguins have special ways of coping with the cold. Mum and Dad have strong claws so they can grip onto the ice. They also have four layers of strong, scaly feathers to keep out the cold.

> Have you been cutting your nails again?

 QUIZ   Penguins use their ***** to grip

After the cold winter ends, Emperor penguins moult and lose some of their feathers. New feathers will grow in their place.

FLiPPeR FaCT

Emperor penguins have small flippers, so they do not lose much heat through them.

Penguin Patrol

In May, Mum lays an egg. Then she goes off to sea to find food. She leaves Dad to look after the egg. The weather is freezing cold so he has to keep it very warm. He covers the egg with a special pouch of skin to keep it warm.

Dad balances the egg on his feet.

DAD HAS NO FOOD FOR UP TO 9 WEEKS WHILE HE LOOKS AFTER THE EGG!

Mum looks after the chick. Now it's Dad's turn to find some food.

12 QUIZ The chick ✶✶✶✶✶✶✶ out of the egg.

At last the chick hatches out of the egg and Mum comes back with the food. Dad passes the chick to Mum. Now it's her turn to babysit! The chick stays in Mum's warm pouch for about two more months. It's still too cold for it to live outside the pouch.

Hurry up, Dad. I'm hungry!

FooD FaCT

Penguins are meat eaters. Mum brings back fish and krill (tiny fish) from her trip.

Penguin Play

The chick is now big and strong enough to live outside the pouch. Mum and Dad leave it while they go off to sea to find food. The chicks are watched over by a few adult penguins in a crèche. There can be thousands of chicks in these penguin play groups!

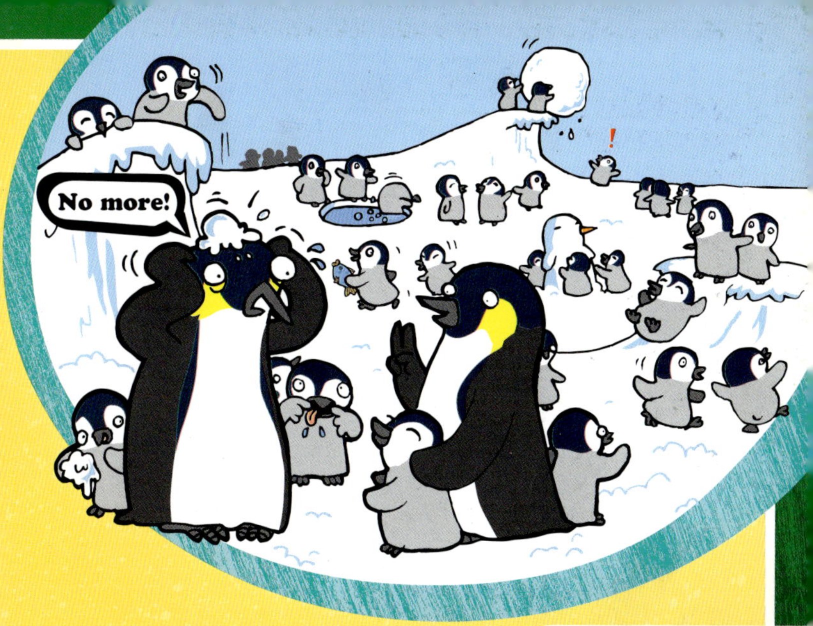

"No more!"

"Don't hurry back, Mum. I'm having fun!"

FiNDiNG FaCt

Penguins can find their chick amongst all the others in a crèche. Parents and chicks call out to each other and they know each other's call.

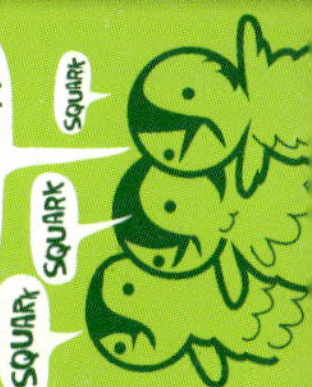

17

Mum and Dad come back with food for the chick. They regurgitate (bring up) the food, which they had stored by eating it. Soon the chick is fully grown and is ready to look after itself. It loses its grey, downy feathers and grows waterproof feathers.

Penguins cannot walk very quickly, so they slide on their tummies to move faster.

18 QUIZ Penguin parents leave their chick in

When it is about five months old, the chick will toboggan down to the sea. Then it will dive deep into the water to find its own fish and krill. In about four years' time it will meet a partner and have a chick of its own!

a ✶✶✶✶✶✶.

Pole to Pole

There are 17 different kinds of penguin, found all over the world. Meet some of the Emperor penguin's relatives!

> The smallest penguin is the Blue penguin, which is not even as big as a ruler!

> The penguin with the coolest haircut is the Macaroni penguin. It has an orange, yellow and black crest on top of its head.

The Chinstrap or Stonecracker penguin is the noisiest penguin. Its call is so loud, it might even crack stones!

The Emperor penguin is the largest penguin in the world. The second largest is the King penguin.

Nearly...

FooT FaCT

Can you guess how the Rockhopper penguin got its name? Well, it hops from rock to rock! Rockhopper penguins build their nests on rocky cliffs, so they need to hop up to them!

Can you work out which of these statements are penguin facts and which are penguin fiction?

True OR False? **Penguins are fish.**  **False**

Penguins are birds. They just like spending lots of time in the sea!

True OR False? **Penguins live near polar bears.** **False**

Penguins live at the South Pole and polar bears live at the North Pole.

  The second largest penguin is the

True OR False? **Penguins are fantastic swimmers.**  True

Penguins are great at swimming and diving and can stay underwater for up to 22 minutes at a time.

True OR False? **Penguins have fur.**  False

Penguins have feathers. Even though chicks look furry, they are actually covered in soft feathers called 'down'.

✶✶✶✶ penguin.